ROBIN PAGE

GARDENING
the Country Way

ILLUSTRATIONS BY
KATHLEEN LINDSLEY

SILENT BOOKS

For my Mother and Father, who in busy lives
found time to keep a real country garden.

First published in Great Britain 1991
by Silent Books, Swavesey, Cambridge CB4 5RA

© Text copyright Robin Page 1991
© Engravings copyright Kathleen Lindsley 1991

ISBN   1 85183 030 8

Typeset by Mews Photosetting
Printed in Great Britain by
St Edmundsbury Press, Bury St Edmunds, Suffolk

CONTENTS

WHY GARDEN?

TODAY there is no need for anybody to have a garden, or work in a garden. Flowers can be bought from wayside kiosks and even the local garage – all of them perfect, scented and already wrapped. Vegetables and fruit too can be purchased from any supermarket, in season and out, already washed, graded and shrink-wrapped – oven ready – and with no trace of dirt, maggot or blemish.

This means that the back garden is redundant; it can be turned into one giant weed-free concrete patio, ideal for sun-lounging, cocktail parties and watching the video. The front can be covered with gravel and turned into a car park for the two BMWs, his and hers. If this is too posh, then the back can just be left and the weeds cut once a year to prevent a confrontation with the neighbours; the front can be used for car repairs –just kick the stones and the oil blotches disappear.

Sadly such gardens can now be seen in both town and country. The idle or misguided owners do not know what they are missing, for the spirit of Man – and Woman – needs a garden; the spirit of Man was created in a garden – the Garden of Eden – and if more people spent time gardening, or simply sitting in a garden, the world would be a better place. Earlier writers agree; Bacon wrote:

> God Almighty first planted a Garden. And indeed it is the Purest of Human pleasures. It is the Greatest Refreshment to the Spirits of Man; Without which, Buildings and Pallaces are but Grosse Handy-works: And a Man shall ever see, that when Ages grow to Civility and Elegance, Men come to Build Stately, sooner then to Garden Finely: As if Gardening were the Greater perfection.

'The garden, too, is the place that can link each person with his or her country past, and this link can be found in a variety of forms, from traditional country garden to inner-city window box. It can show the rhythm of the seasons, the need to reap and sow; and it can give peace, beauty and contentment. It is hardly surprising that Dorothy Frances Gurney wrote:

> The kiss of the sun for pardon,
> The song of the birds for mirth,
> One is nearer God's Heart in a garden
> Than anywhere else on earth.

Gardens can be large or small, it makes no difference, but whatever the size and shape they can provide a private, simple country world of peace and sanity in an increasingly insane, urban world.

I have a small garden. It gives me asparagus, cowslips, plums, apples, tadpoles, birdsong and pleasure. It is a traditional garden. The purpose of this little book is to encourage the reader to enjoy his or her garden in the traditional way: to grow flowers and vegetables, and to be guided by the seasons, country lore, handed-down wisdom and common sense, as well as by orthodox gardening books, garden centres and country nurseries.

Of course having a garden means hard work: 'A Garden's work is never at an end, it begins with the year, and continues to the next'. Perhaps that is it – those people with no interest in gardens are really workshy; I wonder if any politicians are gardeners – I doubt it.

So, because of the work involved, gardening can keep you fit; it is much better than jogging, it has a purpose and you do not look absurd doing it. Before getting the fork, spade or hoe out of the shed it should be remembered that as far as gardening is concerned: 'An hour in the morning is worth two in the evening', and: 'An hour today is worth two tomorrow'.

The gardener who is always going to work 'two hours tomorrow' should also remember 'Little sowing – little reaping' and 'One year's seeding – seven years' weeding'.

The happy gardener needs tools, good tools. I prefer those with traditional wooden handles, not those made from bright, shiny plastic. But be careful: 'Only fools will lend their tools'.

If you lend your tools out, even to friends, they may come back bent, blunt and dirty. Although 'A good day's work can be done with a dirty spade'.

You might also forget who borrowed what – then how do you get the new potatoes when the garden fork has disappeared? – getting the dog to dig them out is not a good idea.

A good garden must include vegetables. Home-grown vegetables always taste better – the drops of sweat simply sweeten the ground. It is also true that 'Everything is good in its season'. These days those urban, shrink-wrapped shoppers, endlessly pushing their supermarket trolleys around, seem to have forgotten that there are such things as seasons; everything is available twelve months a year, with new potatoes for Christmas Day and Brussels sprouts in June. But fruit and vegetables really are better in season; they taste better and they are more natural.

Growing good food has its dangers, however; it can make you eat more, so be warned: 'Gluttony kills more than the sword'.

Some prophets of gloom and doom see disaster looming. 'Why garden?', they ask, 'global warming is taking place – there will be drought and disaster.' Strangely, droughts still enable good crops to be grown, hence: 'Drought never bred death in England' – and 'A dry year never beggars the Master'.

So, with a mixture of tradition, country lore and proverb, I hope to help you enjoy gardening more fully. There is, however, just one proverb that I refuse to quote: 'Wise men make proverbs and fools repeat them'.

TREES, FRUIT AND NUTS

THE GARDEN should not be seen simply as a place to grow the prize begonia, or the giant marrow, it should also be a place of trees, leaves and the fruit they can provide.

HEDGES

Hedges are a vital part of any garden – they give privacy and seclusion and they keep the wind out. Anybody doubting the shelter given by a good hedge should visit the Isles of Scilly – 28 miles south-west of Land's End – the most south-westerly part of Britain. There, the small fields are surrounded by evergreen hedges to keep the strong Atlantic winds at bay, allowing flowers and vegetables to ripen well before those on the mainland.

But the privacy given by hedges in an overcrowded age is important. An Englishman's home may be his castle, but his garden is also his estate, and a good hedge makes a satisfying boundary to that estate. It should also be remembered that 'A hedge between, keeps friendship green' and 'Love thy neighbour, but pull not down thy hedge'.

For several years trendy sociologists, town planners and architects have designed 'open plan' estates with no gardens or boundaries. As a result, these estates also provide 'open season' for discord, upset and friction between neighbours, made worse by a total lack of privacy.

Privet

Privet was often used in the traditional garden hedge, and because it is a good, dense little bush it does give privacy – hence its name.

The hedge at the bottom of my garden contains Hawthorn, Blackthorn, Field Maple, Elder and a wonderful Ivy-covered dead Elm. Ivy should not be removed; it is an attractive plant – giving good cover for birds' nests, as well as providing the last wild flowers of autumn. Only trim it up if it gets too much out of control – don't spray it or kill it.

Holly too makes a fine hedge; it is also excellent for the beautiful Holly Blue butterfly: its caterpillars eat the leaves of both holly and ivy.

Elder

Elder is another wild plant that should not simply be cut out of a hedge as a pest species. Its flowers are attractive, as are its berries –

> Midsummer's near, the elder bloom tells us
> Late summer's gone, the elder fruit knells us.

Both the flower and the berry can be made into good country

wines and cordials. Elder tea can also be made, which is said to be very good for gout.

The most acceptable feature of Elder is the unacceptable smell of its leaves. Not even rabbits eat them – showing the taste to be quite disgusting. Goats are not so fussy – perhaps that helps to explain why Billy goats smell so awful.

A piece of elder stuck among gooseberry bushes prevents the arrival of the magpie moth, and consequently the gooseberry caterpillar. Try the same thing among raspberries to try and reduce the number of maggots in the fruit.

A decoction of elder makes an effective spray against mildew on all fruit trees and strawberries.

TREES

Trees should be grown for their beauty both inside and outside the garden hedge. In my garden, which is a small one, I have silver birch, horse chestnut, elm, lime, ash, plum, apple and pear. Planting trees is about the most unselfish activity that anybody can indulge in; it is the next generation who will see the full beauty of the trees and not the planter, however: 'He that plants trees loves others besides himself'. Similarly – 'Plant pears for your heirs' and 'He who plants a walnut tree expects not to eat the fruit'.

The best time to plant small trees is the autumn: 'you must transplant your trees just about the fall of the leaf – not sooner,

because of the motion of the sap; not later, that they may have
time to take root before the deep frosts'. One old sage instructed:
'Apples, pears, hawthorn, quick oak, set them at All Hallowtide
(All Saints' Day, November 1st) and command them to prosper
– set them at Candlemas (February 2nd) and intreat them to
grow'. That means set them in the autumn – not in the new
year as spring approaches.

There are several other useful old tips concerning tree
planting.

'If a tree be planted in the increase of the Moone, it groweth
to be very great; but if it be in the wane, it will be smaller,
yet a great deal more lasting.'

'Trees which come of nuttes should be sette in the Autumn
at the change or increase of the Moone.'

Another useful instruction is: 'Set trees poor and they will
grow rich, set them rich and they will grow poor. Remove them
out of a more barren into a fatter soil.' For fruit trees, it is
also important to remember: 'Trees often transplanted bear
not much fruit' and 'No sweet apple on a sour stock'.

Trees give shelter, shade, nuts, fruit and wood. This last
harvest is often overlooked, yet nothing can beat a good log
fire on a cold winter's evening.

> Beechwood fires burn bright and clear,
> Hornbeam blazes too,
> If the logs are kept a year,
> To season through and through.
>
> Oak logs will warm you well,
> If they are old and dry;
> Larchwood and pinewood smell,
> But the sparks will fly.
>
> Pine is good, so is yew,
> For warmth through wintry days;
> But poplar, and willow too,
> Take long to dry or blaze.
>
> Birch logs will burn too fast,

Alder scarce at all;
Chestnut logs are good to last,
If cut in the fall.

Holly logs will burn like wax –
You should burn them green;
Elm logs, like smouldering flax,
No flame is seen.

Pear logs and apple logs,
They will scent the room;
Cherry logs across the dogs,
Smell like flowers in bloom.

My favourite wood is apple – it burns well and has a rich, sweet smell. Second must come ash:

Ash dry or ash green,
Makes a fire fit for a queen.

Wood and prunings too thin to use as logs can be stored for use as pea sticks and runner bean poles in the summer. In addition to trees there are several bushes and shrubs that help to make an attractive garden, giving shade, shelter, privacy and blossom; my favourites are juniper, guelder rose, buddleia and lilac. Old countrymen were once good at rhymes – or, more accurately, they once enjoyed making rhymes. 'A cherry year's a merry year: a plum year's a glum year: slow year's a woe year: a haw year's a braw year and an apple year's a drappin year.' The author of this masterpiece in rhyming verse shows why he never became Poet Laureate, but at least he could pair words – just. But every tree mentioned in the rhyme can add both beauty to the garden and fruit or homemade wine to the larder.

Just as chickens 'should not be counted before they are hatched', so fruit should not be counted until it is in the basket: a late frost or a late gale can ruin everything. 'There can be no autumn fruit without spring blossom' and

If apples bloom in March,
For fruit you may search

This means that early blossom is almost certain to be 'cut' by frost.

March is important for another reason: 'He who freely lops in March, will get his lap full of fruit'. (For those who do not understand country English – to lop is to prune.)

The profundity of some of the early wisdom was probably designed to appeal to the local village idiot. Never mind – that ancient wit can now be used for the benefit of town-dwellers and for those ex-urbanites recently moved into the country. Suddenly they realise that fruit and nuts are not made in factories or found in bars of chocolate and so they must learn –

He that would eat the fruit must climb the tree.
He that would eat the kernel must crack the nut – and –
He that sleepeth under a walnut tree doth get himself pains in the head.

Apples

Apples are a pleasure to grow; the blossom is attractive, the fruit is tasty and 'an apple a day keeps the doctor away'. Alternatively: 'Eat an apple going to bed, make the doctor beg his bread'. Care must be taken when harvesting apples:

Pluck fruite to last,
When Michaelmas is past.

> Forget it not, fruit bruised will rot.
> High ladder and long, doth tree least wrong.

Similarly, Thomas Tusser wrote in the sixteenth century:

> Fruit gathered too timely will taste of the woode,
> Will shrinke and be bitter and seldome prooved good.
> So fruit that is shaken or beat off a tree,
> With bruising in falling, soone faultie will bee.

The position of the moon is important in many aspects of gardening, including picking fruit: 'Gather apples, pears and other fruits in the decrease of the Moone'. It is also vital to throw out suspect fruit: 'The rotten apple harms its neighbours', a truism for fruit and people. To prevent small blemishes from turning rotten, it is best to pick apples, and all fruit, when dry. Another interesting observation is: 'Early ripe, early rotten'.

Strangely, tomato plants can help the apple crop. 'A dead tomato plant hung on the bough of an apple tree throughout the winter will preserve it from blight or, better still, the plant should be burnt under the trees, so that the smoke may ascend amongst the branches.'

Other ancient advice preserves fruit trees from the attention of mice and insects. 'Apply in early autumn, around the root, a thick layer of lime and ashes. It would be well to sink the earth around the tree about six or eight inches: throw in a few shovels full of lime and ashes and then cover up with earth and trample it down.'

Plums

Home-grown plums are tasty too; my favourite is the Early River – it confirms that: 'A black plum is as sweet as a white'. The plum grower quickly learns that 'The higher the plum, the riper the plum'. While the other half of this couplet proclaims: 'The richer the cobbler, the blacker his thumb'. Sadly this is no longer true as the traditional cobbler is almost extinct

– replaced by mass-produced throwaway shoes. Some of the best traditional plums and apples are also being replaced by mass-produced, throw-away fruit, and as a result nobody should buy French and Italian plums and apples. They look good but taste like soggy cardboard, or cotton wool. Indeed, I believe that the name of the French Golden Delicious apple actually breaks the Trade Descriptions Act.

Mulberry

Another good fruit tree to grow is the mulberry. The berries of the black mulberry turn a deep wine-red in late summer and are juicy and delicious. Some things even consider the leaves edible, and silkworms favour the leaves of the white mulberry: 'With time and art the leaf of the mulberry-tree becomes satin'. But apart from looking attractive, having valuable leaves and bearing plentiful fruit, the mulberry is also a good indicator of the season. It is the last tree to come into leaf. As soon as the country gardener sees the leaves, he knows that in a normal year his garden will be safe from frost:

> When mulberry trees are green,
> Then no more frosts are seen

The Mulberry is accounted of all other trees the wisest, because it never blossometh til all cold weather be past: so that whensoever you see the Mulberry begin to sprig you may be sure that winter is at an end.

So, as soon as the mulberry leaves appear, it is a sign that work in the vegetable garden can really get under way.

VEGETABLES

I ENJOY growing vegetables, although sadly I never have enough time these days to produce as much as I would like. Once I could grow so many peas, beans, marrows and potatoes, that I even had some left over to sell. I would wheel them up to the local greengrocer for him to sell, in his back garden shed-cum-shop.

Home-grown vegetables always seem to taste better than those bought elsewhere, and it is immensely satisfying to eat and enjoy a completely home-grown meal. It always amazes me that more people do not grow their own vegetables; it is interesting, healthy and, with the sun shining and the birds singing, therapeutic. Instead, Mr and Mrs Average fill their shopping trolleys to overflowing with assorted bags and bundles of carrots and potatoes, plus of course, deep-frozen peas, despite the fact that shopping is boring, unhealthy and can make the participants neurotic.

Many country and suburban gardens could make their owners almost self-sufficient, with surprisingly little effort; yet instead, affluence means that people prefer to buy junk food, and simply grow exotic roses in their gardens.

The traditional country garden produces potatoes, peas, onions, Brussels sprouts and beans – broad, French and runner. An assortment of cabbages and cauliflowers will also be there as well as broccoli, carrots, parsnips, lettuces, radishes and tomatoes. There will be much more besides, making the garden itself look attractive, productive and 'used'. As a result the kitchen table, the larder and the freezer will all be full to overflowing with genuine garden produce.

The proper country gardener should concentrate on the

plants that people once grew for their everyday food; they depended on potatoes – after America had been discovered – cabbages, marrows, onions and peas and beans, both fresh and dried. There are of course some gardeners today who play at gardening – they buy their basics and grow aubergines, peppers, kohl-rabi and calabrese; they impress their friends rather than their stomachs. That really is upper-middle class gardening and consequently there are no country proverbs concerned with the wonders of calabrese and aubergines. I suppose that a modern proverb-provider would have to write:

> If you grow aubergines instead of beans,
> You are upper-middle class it means.

There's nothing wrong with being upper-middle class of course; but if you are, then it is almost certain that you have not experienced the delights of meat pudding and the delicious, but humble swede, or stuffed marrow with broad beans and parsley sauce.

A LOAD OF RUBBISH

Before considering the vegetables to be sown, the good gardener must ensure the fertility and the health of his soil. In the old days that was easy – farmyard 'muck' was always available, in large quantities. In addition, many country cottages also had hens and a pig at the bottom of the garden – all manufacturing what is termed in polite circles 'manure'. Now, sadly, 'muck' or 'manure' is often hard to get, and some country newcomers even consider it to be 'unhygienic'. Fortunately I have a good supply of muck, coming from cow, cockerel, pig and donkey. Those without access to good old farmyard 'muck' should have a compost heap. Everything should go on it – lawn clippings, kitchen waste and even waste paper. Waste paper as compost should not be a surprise – many modern-day newspapers are full of garbage, and garbage makes good compost. The compost should be dug into the garden every autumn.

ROTATION

The other important element for healthy soil is to ensure crop rotation. This helps prevent disease; it rests the soil, and crops such as peas and beans can be used to provide natural nitrogen. To leave areas 'fallow' – to rest them from crop growing completely for a season – is also a good idea.

SOWING

Sowing is probably the most important job in the garden. It requires good judgement, for if the seeds are put in at the wrong time or in the wrong conditions, then there could be no harvest later on. Consequently there are several tried and tested guidelines to ensure success. The most important is:

> This rule in gardening never forget,
> To sow dry and plant wet.

For the benefit of the gardening newcomer, sowing refers to seeds, and planting refers to small plants, i.e. young cabbages.

Whenever I sow dry, once the seeds are safely in, I always water them to ensure that germination begins immediately. Another piece of oral tradition says: 'Sow in the wind'; perhaps it means that rain is blowing up to save watering. Other useful advice includes:

> Early sow,
> Early mow

> Who soweth in raine, hath weede to his paine.
> But worse shall he speed, that soweth ill seed.

With virtually all seeds, apart from potatoes, it is important to sow enough of them. The old adage:

> Four seeds you have to grow,
> One for the rook and one for the crow,
> One to die and one to grow

applies to the garden just as much as it does to the field. In addition to rooks and crows the garden also inevitably loses seeds to voles, mice, sparrows and magpies.

MOON

For years gardeners, farmers, countrymen and mariners have used the moon to forecast the weather. Hence: 'Full moon in October without frost, no frost till full moon in November'; 'A wet month when there are two full moons in it'; 'Clear moon will bring frost soon'; 'If the new moon appear with the points of her crescent turned up, the month will be dry; if the points are turned down it will be wet'.

> Pale moon does rain,
> Red moon does blow,
> White moon does neither rain nor snow.

There is much more. But for years too, farmers and gardeners have also used the moon to help them to decide when to sow. They believe that the position of the moon can affect plants.

Why not? Many people, including some doctors, believe that the moon can affect the behaviour of people:

> When the moon's in the full,
> Then wit's in the wane.

So why shouldn't it affect plants too?

An old great-uncle of mine would always check the state of the moon before planting his beans, saying, 'Set beans in the wane of the moon'. This seemed to confirm a very old piece of country lore:

> Sow peason and beanes in the wane of the moone,
> Who soweth them sooner, he soweth too soone.

Other moon-dictated sowing instructions include: 'At the waning of the February moon, sow onions and leeks. Sow parsley at February full moone'. Also: 'Sow cabbage when the February moon is old'. Some people thought that it helped fertility to do the sowing naked, during a full moon; I have never yet put this theory to the test.

PEAS AND BEANS

Regardless of the state of the moon, peas and beans (broad beans) have many other sowing rules. The reason that peas and beans are involved is simple – at one time they were the staple diet of country people – fresh in the summer and dried in the winter.

Way back in 1525 Sir Anthony Fitzherbert wrote: 'When ye see seasonable time, sow both peas and beanes, so that they be sowen in the bygynnynge of March'. Other once well-known wisdom recommends: 'On Candlemas Day (2 February) stick beans in the clay.' This was seconded by: 'Sow beans in Candlemas Waddle', and almost thirded by:

> On St Valentine's day (14 February), cast beans in clay,
> But on St Chad (2 March), sow good or bad.

Other sages suggested: 'Sow beans in the mud, and they'll grow like wood', and

> David and Chad, sow pease good or bad.

One old writer goes into the subject of beans in much greater detail:

> Beanes may be sowen in Autumne where it is a strong ground, and in the spring in a weake and light grounde. But at what time soever you sowe them, you must have speciall regard to sow them all about the fifteenth daie after the change of the moone, because that in so doing they will be better loaden. They must likewise reape and pull them up in the new of the moone before day. The flowers of beanes not withstanding that they bee of a pleasant and delightsome smell, doe hurt a weake braine, and such a one as is easily carried away and overcome: and hereupon it cometh to passe that there are a great number of fooles when beanes are in flower.

My experience with beans is slightly different. I love the smell of beans on flower – 'on flower' is Cambridgeshire dialect – but my garden has a lot of mice and voles. If your garden is a rodent-free zone, then plant beans early – even in the autumn. If you have many mice, then the beans should be sown late, to allow time for the mice to be lured onto other sprouting things first.

For kidney beans the rules are slightly different:

> When elm leaves are as big as a shillin',
> Plant kidney beans, if to plant 'em you're willin';
> When elm leaves are as big as a penny,
> You must plant kidney beans if you mean to have any

The only problem with this of course is that old shillings and pennies have disappeared, so sadly have most of the elm trees.

VARIOUS HINTS

There are traditional tips for other vegetables too. Potatoes should never be planted too early, to prevent them from becoming frosted. It is always useful to remember:

> Plant your taters when you will,
> They won't come up before April.

The traditional day for planting potatoes is Good Friday. Shallots should be planted on the shortest day of the year and harvested on the longest day of the year.

When cabbages are transplanted they are always vulnerable to the larvae of the cabbage fly. Tinfoil around the roots can offer some protection, as can rags covered with creosote. Sticks of rhubarb buried among freshly planted cabbages prevent clubroot. Creosoted rags are not only good for cabbages but they are also good for deterring the carrot fly. Another way to protect carrots is to crumble up mothballs and put the crumbs in the soil around the young carrots. Fortunately it does not affect the taste. Mothballs can also be suspended in fruit trees large and small to prevent leaf curl – including that on peach trees. As well as mothballs some strong-smelling vegetables can be grown specifically to get rid of unwanted pests (see pests). The good thing about this, is that the surplus leeks, onions and garlic can be eaten:

> Eat leeks in March and garlic in May,
> And all the year the doctors play.

If anybody doubts the wisdom of eating onions because of the smell on their breath, here is one completely useless hint: 'The smell of garlic takes away the smell of onions'. Garlic is also supposed to make a man 'wink, drink and stink'. I like garlic, onions and leeks, and they should have a place in every country garden. One early writer had a different view: 'Let such as love their heads and brain either forbear such things as are obnoxious to the brain, as Garlick, Leeks, Onions: beware of surfeiting and drunkenness'.

Another plant with a more acceptable smell, and taste, is parsley. A flourishing patch of parsley indicates something very interesting:

> Where the mistress is the master;
> The parsley grows faster.

This means that in a garden with plenty of parsley, as soon as the vegetables have been hoed – an order will come, commanding that work should now start in the flower garden.

FLOWERS

IT IS STRANGE – the older I get, the more I appreciate flowers
– in fact Wordsworth described my feelings precisely:

> To me the meanest flower that blows can give
> Thoughts that do often lie too deep for tears.

I love virtually all flowers – in the open field, along a hedgerow,
in marsh, wood and meadow tangle. But I love the flowers of
the garden too, summed up by a country writer many years ago:

> The most pleasant and delectable thing for recreation is our
> flower garden. It is a commendable and seemly thing to
> behold many acres of ground well tilled, but yet it is much
> more to behold faire and comely proportions: delightfull
> borders of lavender, rosemarie, boxe and such other like to
> heare the ravishing musicke of an infinite number of prettie
> small birds: and to smell so sweete a nosegaie so near at
> hand.

THE TRADITIONAL GARDEN

The most attractive flower garden is not the formal fantasy
garden, full of exotic freaks and botanical rarities; it is the traditional simple country garden with hollyhocks and herbs, lilac
and lavender, foxgloves, sunflowers, wallflowers, sweet williams,
night-scented stocks, Michaelmas daisies, daffodils, snowdrops,
crocuses and of course the rose. In addition to these I also love
the peony, which confirms, alas: 'The fairest flowers soonest
fade'. Although the flower fades quickly, fortunately the plant
itself will last a lifetime.

In my garden I also have wild flowers; I never cut my front

lawn until the cowslips have seeded, and my roses are nearly all wild. This wild beauty was best summed up by Rupert Brooke:

> Unkempt about those hedges blows,
> An English unofficial rose.

The one flower I want, but is still missing is the wood anemone – known also by its country name of 'windflower'. The sixteenth-century herbalist John Parkinson described it perfectly: 'The anemones likewise or Windeflowers are so full of variety and so dainty, so pleasant and so delightsome flowers, that the sight of them doth enforce an ernest longing desire in the minde of any one to be a possessour of some of them at least.' Despite his praises, those people wanting wild flowers should not dig them up – they should get them from proper nurseries, many specialise in domesticated 'wild flowers' these days. Consequently it is now possible to have the wild flower delights of meadow or woodland glade, without stealing plants from the wild – which in most cases is illegal anyway.

Today some serious conservationists believe that the wild garden is a new idea; it is not – Francis Bacon (1561–1626) was advocating the wild corner years ago.

> For Gardens . . . ought . . . to be divided into three Parts: A Greene in the Entrance; a Heath or Desart in the Going forth; And the Maine Garden in the midst . . . The Greene hath two pleasures: The one, because nothing is more

Pleasant to the Eye, then Greene Grasse kept finely shorn; The other, because it will give you a Faire Alley in the midst, by which you may go in front upon Stately Hedge, which is to enclose the Garden . . . For the Heath which was the Third Part of our Plot, I wished it to be framed, as much as may be, to a Naturall Wildnesse.

THE FLOWERING YEAR

'Fading flowers find no favour' – so the secret of a good flower garden is to have flowers at all times of the year – from Christmas Roses at the end, to Winter Heliotrope in the beginning, and an assortment of others in between.

Snowdrops are essential as they herald the end of winter and the approach of spring. Their country name is 'Candlemas bells' – suggesting that they should be flowering by 2 February. Snowdrops are also handy for another reason – the bulbs, cut open, can be applied to chilblains with good effect.

April, May and June are wonderful months for flowers, hence:

> April with his hack and bill,
> Plants a flower on every hill.

Sweet April showers do spring Maie flowers.
Gather sweet briar in June, for it promoteth cheerfulness.

Every month has its flowers; even November, usually agreed
as the dullest month of the year, can often still have chrysanthemums – 'Gather November gold when you may'.

PLANTING FLOWERS

In exactly the same way that the moon is thought to help the
vegetable garden, so flowers are also thought to be affected by
the moon.

> The seeds from which you expect to have double Flowers,
> must be sown at the full of the Moon, or in two or three
> days after. It hath been long observed that the Moon hath
> great influence over Plants (over Animals it is very con-
> spicuous). And if it hath any such influence, then surely it
> is in the doubling of Flowers.

Some flowers also have definite rules associated with them. 'Set
sage in May; it will grow alway' and 'plant honeysuckle with
its roots in the shade and its flowers in the sun'. If sweet peas
are planted on St Patrick's Day they are said to grow large.
I am afraid that I don't like sweet peas and so I do not grow
them, large or small.

The Americans have a knack of inventing words and incor-
porating them into the English language. One of these is
'symbiotic' – things, including plants, have symbiotic relationships – it means that one species benefits from, or needs another.
I prefer to use a softer expression – they can have 'linked'
relationships. One of these plants is the marigold – if planted
with potatoes and tomatoes, yield seems to improve and some
common pests are kept at bay. Foxgloves have the same effect
on potatoes, tomatoes and apples, and make them keep better.
Cabbages too benefit from having herbs planted near them,
which means that the flower garden can spread into the

vegetable garden. Soft fruit also benefits – strawberries grow better if borage or beans are planted near them. A linked relationship of a different kind involves the crocus and lavender. If crocuses are planted near lavender, the birds are said to leave them alone.

ROSES

If some people and things find lavender unpleasant, the rose on the other hand must be universally admired for both its fragrance and its beauty. But as usual things are not always straightforward: 'The sweetest rose grows upon the sharpest thorn'. Roses may be difficult to pick, but blight, aphids and mildew like them and spoil them quickly. A clove of garlic planted nearby provides another linked relationship and will keep off greenfly. Somehow it also helps to improve the scent. Half a pound of tobacco in a gallon of water, painted onto the leaves, will get rid of aphids. The mixture should be rinsed off afterwards. An equal mixture of sulphur and tobacco dust sprinkled onto rose leaves, when the dew is still on them, will get rid of blight. When the problem is checked a decoction of elder leaves should be syringed over the infected parts.

DAFFODILS

Just as every garden should have roses, so it should also have daffodils. A spring without daffodils is unimaginable – like happiness without a smile. Everybody knows Wordsworth's lines about daffodils, but Shakespeare loved them too:

> Daffodils, that come before the swallow dares, and take
> The winds of March with beauty;

My favourite poem is 'To Daffodils' by Robert Herrick:

> Fair daffodils, we weep to see
> You haste away so soon

As yet the early-rising sun
Has not attained his noon.
Stay, stay
Until the hasting day
Has run
But to the evensong;
And having prayed together, we
Will go with you along.

The good thing about daffodils is that they are easy to grow and need little attention.

TULIPS

For some reason beyond my comprehension, some people put tulips alongside daffodils for beauty and as a harbinger of spring. The otherwise sensible John Parkinson was a great admirer of tulips.

To tell you of all the sorts of Tulipes (which are the pride of delight) they are so many, and as I may say almost infinite, doth both passe my ability, and as I believe the skill of any other . . . Besides this glory of variety in colors that these flowers have, they carry so stately and delightfull a forme, and do abide so long in their bravery that there is no Lady or Gentlewoman of any worth that is not caught with this delight.

Many people agree with him; sadly, I disagree. I have never

liked tulips – they look too regimented and artificial. Consequently there is not one tulip in my garden – Tulips from Amsterdam ought to stay there. In fact my views correspond with those of Thomas Fuller in 1650:

> There is lately a Flower (shall I call it so? in courtesie I will tearme it so, though it deserve not the appellation) a Toolip, which hath engrafted the love and affections of most people unto it; and what is this Toolip? a well-complexion'd stink, an ill favour wrapt up in pleasant colours.

HERBS

Are herbs flowers? Whether they are or not, every garden should have them, either in a special herb garden, or spread about the garden in general. Rosemary, thyme, tarragon, lovage, mint and many more. Sage too is important;

> He that would live for aye,
> Must eat sage in May.

Herbs look attractive; their scents are a delight; they can improve cookery; they can sweeten household air and they have a place in home herbal medicine. Those wanting to dabble in country cures should read the old herbalists Culpeper and Gerard, for both information and amusement. For instance, on the foxglove, Culpeper wrote: 'I am confident that anointment of it is one of the best remedies for a scabby head'. While Gerard believed: 'Foxglove boiled in water or wine, and drunken, doth cut and consume the thick toughnesse of grosse slimie flegme and naughtie humours'. Fortunately I do not suffer from naughtie humours and so my herbs are simply grown for the pleasure of having them in the garden, and in the cooking pot. A good way of ensuring a healthy herb garden is to have a sharp pair of garden shears:'You may yet clip lavender, thyme, pennyroyal, sage, rosemary, etc. and the oftener you clip and cut them, the more they will thrive'.

BUTTERFLIES AND BEES

Butterflies and bees are, of course, not flowers. But they give colour and beauty to any garden. I would never dream of name dropping, but I remember Prince Charles describing butterflies to me on one occasion as being 'like mobile flowers'. His analogy coincides with the view of W.H. Davies – that brilliant but underrated tramp-cum-hobo-cum-poet. His poem 'Flying Blossoms' says it all:

> These Butterflies, in twos and threes,
> That flit about in wind and sun –
> See how they add their flowers to flowers,
> And blossom where a plant has none!

Many flowers and shrubs attract butterflies – their scent promising nectar – buddleia is known as the 'butterfly bush' and polyanthus, wallflower, thrift, honesty, aubrietia, lavender, golden rod, cornflower, and Michaelmas daisy are among the many plants and flowers that are all good for butterflies, and add beauty to the garden too.

Bees should also be welcomed. They are a sign of a good, healthy, sweet-smelling garden; they help the gardener in his work by pollinating his fruit and vegetables – from early plums to late runner beans. So remember the old rule: 'Don't go to law with your Neighbour, because his bees suck honey from your Flowers'. Bees and butterflies should be welcomed into the garden like old friends, and chemical sprays should be used with extreme caution when they are flying.

THE SCENTED GARDEN

Butterflies and bees like a scented garden, and that is the final essential element of the perfect country garden. Again Francis Bacon summed it up well:

> And because the breath of flowers is farre sweeter in the Aire (where it comes and goes like the Warbling of Musick) than in the hand, therefore nothing is more fit for that delight than to know what be the Flowers and Plants that doe best perfume the Aire. Roses Damask and Red are fast Flowers of their Smells, so that you may walke by a whole row of them and find nothing of their Sweetnesse; yea, though it may be a Morning's Dew. Bayes likewise yeeld no Smell as they grow; Rosemary little; nor Sweet-Marjoram. That which above all others yeelds the Sweetest Smell in the Aire is the Violet; specially the White-double Violet, which comes twice a yeare about the middle of Aprill, and about Bartholomew-tide. Next to that is the Muske Rose; then the Strawberry-Leaves dying, with a most excellent Cordiall Smell. Then the Flower of the Vines; it is a little dust, like the dust of a Bent, which growes upon the Cluster in the first coming forth. Then Sweet Briar. Then Wall-Flowers, which are very Delightfull, to be set under a parlour or Lower Chamber Window. Then Pincks and Gilly-Flower, specially the Matted Pinck and Clove Gilly-Flower. Then the Flowers of the Lime Tree. Then the Honeysuckles, so they be somewhat a farre off. Of beane Flowers I speak not, because they are field Flowers. But those which perfume the Aire most delightfully, not passed by as the rest, but being Trodden upon and Crushed, are Three: that is Burnet, Wild-Time, and Water Mints. Therefore you are to set whole Allies of them, to have the Pleasure when you walke or tread.

The two other fragrances I would have included are those of apple blossom and lilac.

PESTS

EVERY GARDEN has pests, from next door's cat rolling in the onion bed, to aphids and mildew. My worst enemy is the flea beetle; whatever I do it seems to regard my garden as a special reserve for flea beetles. With this in mind they chomp away happily on my recently germinated young cabbages and brussels sprouts, and whatever I do, they seem to thrive. As a result I have to sprinkle liberal quantities of derris powder over my infant plants; the choice is simple – I either use the derris powder, or I have no green vegetables.

My other great problem is slugs. Everything in the garden that I like they like too, particularly young peas and beans. It is the conservationist's dilemma – can you love a slug? And if they were rare, would you want to preserve them?

Fortunately there are many ways of getting rid of slugs that avoid the use of slug bait or pellets. Slug bait can be a tremendous danger to both pets and wildlife; one of my saddest experiences was to lose a much-loved dog after it ate a neighbour's poisonous slug mixture.

The safest and simplest way to get rid of slugs is to put slices of turnip around the garden on a summer, or autumn evening. This will attract slugs in large numbers and they can be carted away. Cabbage leaves, heated in an oven until they are soft and then covered with unsalted butter or fresh dripping, are just as effective.

Fresh, dry ash from the fire, put around the edge of the garden, can deter slugs, as they do not like crossing dry, fine particles. The problem is that ash absorbs moisture quickly and soon ceases to be dry and fine. One old writer was quite neurotic about slugs and seems to have become an advocate of slug hunting.

> Slugs and Snails are great enemies to every kind of garden-plant, whether flower or vegetable; they wander in the night to feed, and return at day-light to their haunts; the shortest and surest direction is, 'rise early, catch them, and kill them'. If you are an early riser, you may cut them off from their day retreats, or you may lay cabbage leaves about the ground, especially on the beds which they frequent. Every morning examine these leaves, and you will find a great many taking refuge beneath; if they plague you very much, search for their retreat, which you can find by their slimy track, and hunt there for them day by day.

The same writer had another plan for snails. 'Snails are particularly fond of bran; if a little is spread on the ground, and covered over with a few cabbage-leaves or tiles, they will congregate under them in great numbers, and by examining them every morning, and destroying them, their numbers will be materially decreased.'

Although this old gardener disliked snails, I actually like them – they can be attractive to look at and they make excellent thrush food. They can also be good weather indicators. When snails climb up the stalks of grass it is said to indicate rain, as does the appearance of black snails. In addition: 'If snails come out in February, they will stay at home in March'. Consequently I am reluctant to remove a natural weather forecasting aid from my garden.

Moles can also be weather forecasters and if they throw up more earth than usual, rain is again indicated. However, moles can be a problem in the garden and molehills among the lettuces are a nuisance, and in the middle of the lawn they can be a disaster. I don't like the idea of killing moles and so rags soaked in creosote, put in their runs, usually persuade them to move on – carbide, mothballs and onions all have the same effect. Another trick is to place a few empty bottles in the soil or lawn with just their necks showing – small beer bottles are ideal. The moles will quickly go. The wind in the neck of the bottle probably sounds rather like a foghorn to a mole busily working underground.

Caper spurge is another mole deterrent. It was once known as the 'mole plant'. It is thought that moles dislike the plant's root secretion. One old gardener gives some totally useless information about moles. 'The mole when at rest bears more resemblance to a stuffed bag than a living animal'. How interesting. I know a gardener-cum-hedge-layer who has a stuffed mole on his hat; the fashion has not caught on.

FOUR-LEGGED PESTS

Other four-legged visitors and residents can also be a gardener's nightmare. I cannot plant beans in the autumn as the mice and voles take every one, with a small, tidy hole dug directly above each bean. The way to overcome this problem is to plant

holly leaves with the beans and peas. Soaking them with paraffin is an alternative solution.

Rats can be another unpleasant menace. The crushed roots of bryony put down their holes will drive them away.

DEER AND BADGERS

Deer, from small muntjac to large red, and badgers can create havoc in a garden. Deer love your favourite roses and badgers are not fussy – they will eat most of your fruit, vegetables and bulbs. The liberal use of creosote is again one solution, although the smell on a warm summer's day will be unpleasant for you as well as for the would-be visitors. If fences are erected, they must be tall, to stop the deer jumping over – and buried, to stop the badgers digging underneath.

Rabbits are diggers, jumpers and squeezers through small holes, so try a border of onions, it will often persuade them to search elsewhere for their supper. The presence of cats will deter rabbits, and liberal helpings of sprinkled pepper will help to deter the cats from rolling in the onion bed, or worse, relieving themselves among the small carrots. Cotton criss-crossed tightly will also keep cats off.

TWO-LEGGED INTRUDERS

For some peculiar reason sparrows are very fond of beetroot. Criss-crossed cotton can again be used to keep them off – nylon being strong and non-biodegradable should not be used in case the birds become entangled in it.

For those with an artistic bent, potato hawks can be made, to strike terror in sparrows and pigeons. Feathers should be stuck into a large baking potato to look like the wings and tail of a predatory bird. This flying 'murphy hawk' should then be suspended by a length of string. A friend with a vivid imagination claims that his hawks are extremely effective.

Scarecrows and flapping strips of plastic are good until the birds become accustomed to them. Pigeons in the early morning can be a nuisance with sprouting peas. I do not like killing things, but pigeon pie with new potatoes and new peas makes a very acceptable solution to the problem.

Magpies and jays will eat fruit – even unripe gooseberries. They can be very greedy. 'One cherry tree suffices not two jays.' I fire off my ancient twelve-bore shotgun near magpies and they soon get the message.

Magpies can be easily caught in humane traps. Those people who cannot face killing them, should release them into places that deserve more magpies, e.g. Milton Keynes, Slough, Cumbernauld, etc. etc.

MULTI-LEGGED INVADERS

Aphids

In warm years, aphids – greenfly, white fly and black fly – can reach plague proportions. Among broad beans the affected parts of the plant should be broken off, as soon as the creatures appear. An effective spray can be made from 2½ lb of elder leaves boiled in 2 gallons of water. Liquid fertiliser made in the same way with nettles is also good, or rather bad, for aphids, and can be used against mildew for good measure; mildew on cabbages and sprouts can be sprayed with methylated spirits. If no spray is at hand the aphids can simply be sprayed off with a jet of cold water. Caterpillars on the cabbages can be given the same treatment. Garlic, onions and leeks keep aphids away, and lack of aphids seem to be another mysterious bonus from growing marigolds.

Grubs, bugs, beetles and borers

Soft soap rubbed onto young fruit trees deters bugs, beetles and moths. When it rains the soap then runs into the soil and promotes growth. Hard soap can be used to kill various borers in trees – by blocking up their bored-out holes. For an assortment of grubs, old gardeners had a rather dramatic solution – a smoky fire blowing through the fruit trees and gooseberry bushes. The offending munchers roll up into a ball and fall off their favourite trees and bushes.

Leaf lice

The first necessity for dealing with leaf lice is to find a book that explains the old forms of measurement, then mix an ounce of flowers of sulphur with one bushel of sawdust. The mixture should be scattered liberally over the infected plants.

Earwigs, ants and wasps

I tolerate all three of these in my garden – the secret with wasps is just to get to the fruit before they do. In days gone by some gardeners tended to get rather neurotic, particularly about earwigs.

Earwigs are very destructive insects; their favourite food is the petals of roses, pinks, dahlias, and other flowers. They may be caught by driving stakes into the ground, and placing on each an inverted flower pot; the earwigs will climb up and take refuge under it, when they may be taken out and killed. Clean bowls of tobacco-pipes placed in like manner on the tops of smaller sticks are very good traps; or very deep holes may be made in the ground with a crowbar, into these they will fall, and may be destroyed by boiling water.

When I garden I prefer to use boiling water to make cups of tea.

Just as some pests go straight for the flowers, or vegetables, others settle directly onto the gardener. Consequently the working gardener can be bombarded by flies, midges and mosquitoes. The crushed leaves of herb robert keep most things off, the disadvantage being that it makes you smell rather like an old billy goat. A chamomile brew rubbed over all bare skin will keep most things off, as will a garland of bryony.

NATURAL PEST CONTROL

In nature there are many natural pest controllers, and so a good wildlife garden will also be a garden where fewer sprays and traps have to be used. The best mousetrap is an owl, and old trees will attract them in. Old trees will also find favour with woodpeckers, to peck up an assortment of bugs, beetles and ants. Thrushes will go for snails, blackbirds for slugs, starlings for leatherjackets and assorted tits for assorted bugs and caterpillars. Another indispensable slug eater is the hedgehog, and bats make good mobile moth traps.

Ladybirds, ground beetles, hoverflies and lacewings will scoff aphids, and frogs and toads will go for many harmful creepy crawlies, including slugs. So if your garden has an owl, a thrush,

a blue tit, and a frog, many potential pests will find themselves transformed into a tasty snack. Old gardeners may not have liked earwigs, but they certainly liked toads:

> Toads are among the best friends the gardener has; for they live almost exclusively on the most destructive kinds of vermin. Unsightly, therefore, though they may be, they should on all accounts be encouraged; they should never be touched nor molested in any way; on the contrary, places of shelter should be made for them to which they may retire from the burning heat of the sun. If you have none in your garden, it will be quite worth your while to search for them in your walks, and bring them home, taking care to handle them tenderly, for although they have neither the will nor the power to injure you, a very little rough treatment will injure them; no cucumber or melon frame should be without one or two.

A keen gardener of my acquaintance hasn't got a toad, but he's got several frogs in his greenhouse – they are plump, and as a result the gardener has no insect or bug trouble. These days frogs and toads should not be captured in the wild – the right conditions should be created in the hope that they will turn up. Bits of corrugated iron, or wood, left in long grass will provide them with shelter and concealment away from the greenhouse.

WEEDS

WHAT is a weed? In general a weed is simply a wild plant, including wild flowers, growing in the wrong place. Unfortunately my garden has plenty of wild plants growing in the wrong place, for 'weeds want no sowing' and 'There is no garden without its weeds'. The other unfortunate fact is that the better the land, the larger and more flourishing the weeds: 'Fat land grows the foulest weeds'. Most weeds can be controlled simply, with the hoe. But the job must not be put off for another day as 'One year's seeding' definitely is 'seven years' weeding'.

Unfortunately there are a few weeds that really are weeds, and once they take hold they are very difficult to eradicate. The worst weed of all is couch grass, known also as twitch.

Indeed, if twitch was a crop, I would have the most productive garden on the planet. Its sharp, pointed roots run everywhere and can grow right through a potato. If you chop a piece of twitch into fifty pieces, you get fifty plants instead of one. Sadly, the best way to get rid of twitch, and the equally troublesome ground elder, is to spray them with some noxious poison, but unfortunately, such drastic action puts that part of the garden out of action for a time. Even then, if it is a wet season, the poisoned and 'dead' twitch is so resilient that it will start to sprout again.

One natural treatment can be tried. Twitch seems to dislike lupins, tomatoes and turnips – yes, turnips – so they should be planted in large quantities until the twitch disappears. The most efficient twitch control, however, is a bent back; it should be pulled out of freshly dug soil, not simply turned over or hoed.

The only friends of twitch are dogs and children. Dogs eat it when they are feeling one degree under, hence the country name of 'Dog's Grass'. Children like it, as pressed between the thumbs it makes a simple whistle. If dogs are the real friends of twitch then the great friends of ground elder are said to be Bishops. Apparently, at one time, certain high-living Bishops favoured it for combating gout. Consequently ground elder is also known as Bishop's Weed.

Other weeds that can take over the garden are creeping

buttercup, field bindweed, or bellvine, and cleavers, or goosegrass. Bindweed is a real nightmare weed; its roots go so deep that two of its alternative names are hell weed and devil's guts.

THISTLES

Thistles can be troublesome weeds, although left in a wild corner they can be attractive, and butterflies love them. Old-time gardeners would cut their thistles with a 'stub' – so:

> Stub a thistle in May, it will be back the next day,
> Stub a thistle in June, it will be back soon,
> Stub a thistle in July, it will surely die.

This is a very wise guide, for early thistles are very difficult to kill. Another piece of well-tried country lore warns:

> Cut your thistles before St John [24 June],
> And you'll have two instead of one.

One way to combat thistles, coltsfoot and bracken is to roll them regularly with a heavy metal roller when they are young. If hand weeding with thistles is attempted, remember: 'He that handles thorns shall prick his fingers'; similarly: 'He that handles a nettle tenderly is soonest stung'.

NETTLES

Nettles can be both a help and a hindrance. If they are weeded by hand, the weeder must grip them quickly and firmly and grab the stem and the back of the leaves. However, few hardy people now weed with unprotected hands, and good leather gloves will protect from both nettles and thistles. If the brave tackle stinging nettles unprotected, then:

> When your fingers nettles find,
> Be sure a dock is close behind.

A dock leaf rubbed onto the sting will bring relief.

I remove nettles growing among my vegetables, but I leave them around my gooseberries. In fact they can also be left around redcurrants and blackcurrants, as they offer some shelter and protection from late frosts. Nettles also seem to keep soft fruit more disease-free, and they improve the quality of the soil. Soil cleared of nettles is usually very pliable and fertile.

Young nettles need not be made into compost, they can be eaten – boiled, they taste like spinach and are delicious. I deliberately leave several clumps of nettles each year as many insects love to eat their leaves, including the caterpillars of the small tortoiseshell, peacock and comma butterflies; so the nettle is an important butterfly plant.

HORSERADISH

This is another 'weed' that can be left in small clumps. The root, made into horseradish sauce, is a must when eating beef. Like onions, horseradish makes the eyes stream with tears when it is being ground up.

WEATHER FORECASTING

Some weeds can also be left as weather forecasting aids. The most well known is the small, attractive Scarlet Pimpernel – known as the Poor Man's Weatherglass. In good weather the flower is open, but as rain approaches, it closes. Trefoil and clover will contract their leaves at the approach of a storm. Marigolds and wood sorrel behave in a similar way.

WEEDS AS FLOWERS

Sadly, many people regard some quite acceptable wild flowers as 'weeds'. I like to see weeds left as wild flowers – blackberries in the hedge, meadowsweet by the ditch, cow parsley left as 'Queen Anne's Lace', and buttercups, daisies and cowslips left in the lawn. A true country garden is made more attractive by the presence of daisies in the lawn – a green lawn, devoid of everything except grass, seems to suggest sterile soil and sterile minds.

Wild flowers in the lawn not only improve the appearance, but they also allow a number of traditional country wild flower games to be played: the reflection of a buttercup on the cheek or chin to prove a liking for butter; plantain – that can be made into catapult guns; the wonder of dandelion clocks; the excitement of finding a four-leaved clover and of course, daisy chains. Daisy chains have been worn by countless generations of country girls as necklaces and hairbands. Not only are they fun to make but:

> Girls who wear a daisy chain,
> Grow up pretty, never plain.

Surely that is a good enough reason never to destroy another daisy?

SAINTS' DAYS AND SPECIAL DAYS

THROUGHOUT the year there are a number of special days, often linked to the Church calendar, which are of help to the keen, traditional gardener. Some have been mentioned already and a few I will mention again. Although not always accurate, they come from generations of gardening and weather-watching countryfolk and so should be taken seriously.

The first significant date of the year is, appropriately enough, January 1st – then, daylight lengthens as far as a cock's crow carries. This also means that you can work in the garden for an extra minute.

As the days get even longer, remember:

> As the day lengthens
> So the cold strengthens

Make sure your seed potatoes and your dahlias are protected against the frost. By the last day of the month, January 31st, hazel catkins should be out.

Candlemas Day – February 2nd

This is a very important day for weather forecasting, farming and gardening:

> On Candlemas Day if the thorns hang a drop,
> You will be sure of getting a good pea crop

If the weather changes, beware: 'Change of weather finds discourse for fools'.

St Matthias – February 24th

This St Matthias, Mathie or Matthes, must not be confused with the Apostle St Matthew – his special day is September

21st. This one is surrounded by mystery. Some believe that he spread the Gospel and was martyred in Palestine; others that he preached and died in Ethiopia. However, whatever he did and wherever he did it, he is important in the gardening year: 'St Mathie sends sap into the tree' and 'St Matthew breaks the ice – if he finds none he will make it'.

St David – March 1st; St Chad – March 2nd

> Sow peas and beans on David and Chad,
> Whether the weather be good or bad.

Easter

Easter is a 'moveable feast' – but:

> Plant potatoes on Maundy Thursday
> Turnips on St Margaret's Day (20 July)

This, of course, is a day earlier than those who claim that the best potatoes are planted on Good Friday.

By the end of March the temperature should be rising –

> On St Joseph's Day [29 March],
> Fling the warming pan away.

Also remember:

> March winds and April showers,
> Bring forth May flowers.

All Fools' Day – April 1st

If it thunders on All Fools' Day,
It brings good crops of corn and hay.

Be sure not to sow your beans and peas upside down on this day.
Whatever the month – the full moon brings fair weather.

April 19th is Primrose Day

St Dunstan's Day – May 19th

For those with the supernatural lurking at the bottom of their
garden this day is interesting:

From your apple trees keep the witches away,
Or they'll blight the bloom on St Dunstan's Day.

May can give a clue to the quality of the fruit and vegetables
later on:

A dry May and a dripping June,
Brings all things into tune.

June is a good month – there are few special days to remember
and so more time can be spent simply sitting in the garden,
enjoying it. However, on June 21st shallots should be harvested
and:

Bonfires lit on midsummer night,
Shall fill the apple lofts up tight.

This could simply be the smoke knocking out the bugs and grubs
at exactly the right time.

St John's Day – June 24th

Cut your thistles before St John,
You will have two instead of one.

On the eve of St John – July 23rd – hazel should be cut for
divining rods.

St Swithin's Day – July 15th

July is the dreaded month that contains St Swithin's Day. It is a day that I take very seriously and I hope desperately for a rain-free day. If I feel just one or two drops I even pretend that it is not rain but an incontinent gnat flying by. One of the several verses relating to St Swithin's is:

> St Swithin's Day, if thou dost rain,
> For forty days it will remain.
> St Swithin's Day, if they be fair,
> For forty days 'twill rain nae mair.

There is some hope luckily:

> All the tears St Swithin can cry,
> St Bartholomew's mantle will wipe dry [24 August]

July is a sad month, because of St Mary Magdalene's Day – July 22nd – roses are said to begin to fade on this day. This is the first hint of autumn's approach.

August is a busy month in the garden – therefore every day is a special day. The year continues to move on too:

In August the summer is spelling farewell.

Holy Cross Day – September 14th

Holy Cross Day is also known as Nut-Crack Day, when country people should go 'a-nutting'.

St Matthew's Day – September 21st

On St Matthew's Day there will often be a chill in the air as autumn advances still more:

> St Matthew brings the cold rain and dew.
> St Matthew shuts up the bee.

St Michael's Day – Michaelmas Day – September 29th

This is another important day in the country calendar:

> At Michaelmas Time, or a little before,
> Half an apple goes to the Core.

If St Michael bring thunder, rough weather will follow. Never eat blackberries after Michaelmas Day, as the Devil spits on them. Throughout the month those with fruit in the garden should recite:

> September blowe soft,
> Till fruite be in loft

St Luke's Day – October 18th

If the summer has been a bad one, this date is important. It usually gives a spell of good weather known as St Luke's Little Summer.

All Saints' Day – November 1st

November 1st is a key pointer to the weather of the winter:

> If Ducks do Slide at Hollantide,
> At Christmas they will swim.
> If Ducks do swim at Hollantide,
> At Christmas they will slide.

St Martin's Day – November 11th

Another piece of weather-lore, useful to the gardener, comes on November 11th: if St Martin wears a white band, you may expect a very hard winter. Also, on St Martin's Day, winter is on its way.

St Edmund's Day – November 20th

> Set garlicke and pease,
> St Edmund to please.

St Clement's Day – November 23rd

By St Clement's Day the good gardener will still have some chrysanthemums – the clever gardener will even be able to spell them. Chrysanths were dedicated to St Clement and are known as Clement's Marigolds.

As far as I am concerned December is not a good month for gardening. On December 21st, the shortest day, shallots should be planted. Indicators for next year's crops should also be noticed:

> If the milky way in December shows clear,
> You may safely count on a fruitful year.

If fruit trees are covered with snow on Christmas morning, they will be covered with fruit in the summer.

Christmas Day is important for another reason – the season has turned – spring is coming:

Daylight lengthens to the extent of a gnat's yawn.

A CALENDAR OF GARDENING

A Gardener's guide from the past

JANUARY

Flower of the month – Christmas Rose

Indoor preparations for future operations must be made, as in this month there are only five hours a day available for outdoor work, unless the season be unusually mild. Mat over tulip-beds, begin to force roses. Pot over sea-kale and plant dried roots of border flowers in mild weather. Take strawberries in pots into the greenhouse. Prune and plant gooseberry, currant, fruit and deciduous trees and shrubs. Cucumbers and melons should be sown in the hot bed. Apply manures.

FEBRUARY

Flowers of the month – Snowdrop and Violet

Transplant pinks, carnations, sweet williams, candytuft, campanulas, etc., sweet and garden peas and lettuce, for succession of crops, covering the ground with straw. Sow also savoys, leeks and cabbages. Prune and nail walnut trees, and towards the end of the month plant stocks for next year's grafting, also cuttings of poplar, elder, willow-trees, for ornamental shrubbery. Sow fruit and forest tree seeds.

MARCH

Flower of the month – Primrose

'Spring flowers' to be sown. Border flowers to be planted out. Tender annuals to be potted out under glass. Mushroom beds to be made. Sow artichokes, windsor beans, and cauliflowers for autumn; lettuces and peas for succession of crops, onions, parsley, radishes, savoys, asparagus, red and white cabbages, and beet; turnips, early broccoli, parsnips and carrots. Plant slips and parted roots of perennial herbs. Graft trees and protect early blossoms. Force rose-tree cuttings under glass.

APRIL

Flower of the month – Cowslip

Sow for succession peas, beans and carrots; parsnips, celery and sea-kale, spring flowers. Plant evergreens, dahlias, chrysanthemums, and the like, also potatoes, slips of thyme, parted roots, lettuces, cauliflowers, cabbages, onions. Lay down turf, remove caterpillars. Sow and graft camellias, and propagate and graft fruit and rose trees by all the various means in use. Sow cucumbers and vegetable marrows for planting out. **This is the most important month in the year for gardeners.**

MAY

Flower of the month – Hawthorn

Plant out your seedling flowers as they are ready, and sow again for succession larkspur, mignonette, and other spring flowers. Pot out tender annuals. Remove auriculas to a north easterly aspect. Take up bulbous roots as the leaves decay. Sow kidney beans, broccoli for spring use, cape for autumn, cauliflowers for December; Indian corn, cress, onions (to plant out as bulbs next year), radishes, aromatic herbs, turnips, cabbages, savoys, lettuces, etc. Plant celery, lettuces, and annuals; thin spring crops. Stick peas, etc. Earth up potatoes. Moisten mushroom beds.

JUNE

Flowers of the month – Waterlily and Honeysuckle

Sow giant stocks to flower next spring. Slip myrtles to strike, and lay pinks, carnations, roses and evergreens. Plant annuals in borders, and auriculas in shady places. Sow kidney beans, pumpkins, cucumbers for pickling, and (late in the month) endive and lettuces. Plant out cucumbers, marrows, leeks, celery, broccoli, cauliflowers, savoys, and seedlings, and plants propagated by slips. Earth up potatoes. Cut herbs for drying when in flower.

JULY

Flowers of the month – Rose and Carnation

Part auricula and polyanthus roots. Take up summer bulbs as they go out of flower, and plant saffron crocus and autumn bulbs. Gather seeds. Clip evergreen borders and hedges, strike myrtle slips under glass. Net fruit trees. Finish budding by the end of the month. Head down espaliers. Sow early dwarf cabbages to plant out in October for spring; also endive, onions, kidney beans for late crop, and turnips. Plant celery, endive, lettuces, cabbages, leeks, strawberries, and cauliflowers. Stick peas. Tie up salads. Earth celery. Take up onions for drying.

AUGUST

Flowers of the month – Harebell and Mallow

Sow flowers to bloom indoors in winter, and pot all young stocks raised in the greenhouse. Sow early red cabbages, cauliflowers for spring and summer use, cos and cabbage lettuce for winter crop. Plant out winter crops. Dry herbs and mushroom spawn. Plant out strawberry roots, and net currant trees, to preserve the fruit through the winter.

SEPTEMBER

Flowers of the month – Clematis, or Traveller's Joy,
Arbutus, and Meadow Saffron

Plant crocuses, scaly bulbs, and evergreen shrubs.
Propagate by layers and cuttings all herbaceous plants,
currant, gooseberry, and other fruit trees. Plant out
seedling pinks. Sow onions for spring planting, carrots,
spinach, and Spanish radishes in warm spots. Earth up
celery. House potatoes and edible bulbs. Gather pickling
cucumbers. Make tulip and mushroom beds.

OCTOBER

Flowers of the month – China-aster, Holly and Ivy

Sow rose-tree seeds and fruit stones, also larkspurs and
the hardier annuals to stand the winter, also hyacinths
and smooth bulbs, in pots and glasses. Plant young trees,
cuttings of jasmine, honeysuckle, and evergreens. Sow
mignonette for pots in winter. Plant cabbages, etc., for
spring. Cut down asparagus, separate roots of daisies,
irises, etc. Trench, drain, and manure.

NOVEMBER

Flowers of the month – Laurestine and Wych Hazel

Sow sweet peas for an early crop. Take up dahlia roots.
Complete beds for asparagus and artichokes. Plant dried
roots of border flowers, daisies, etc. Take potted
mignonette indoors. Set strawberries. Sow peas, leeks,
beans, and radishes. Plant rhubarb in rows. Prune hardy
trees, and plant stocks of fruit trees. Store carrots, etc.
Shelter from frost where it may be required. Plant shrubs
for forcing. Continue to trench and manure
vacant ground.

DECEMBER

Flowers of the month – Cyclamen and Winter Aconite.
(Holly berries are now available for floral decoration.)

Continue in open weather to prepare vacant ground for
spring, and to protect plants from frost. Cover bulbous
roots with matting. Dress flower borders. Prepare forcing
ground for cucumbers, and force asparagus and sea-kale.
Plant gooseberry, currant, apple and pear trees. Roll grass
plots if the season be mild and not too wet. Prepare poles,
stakes, pea-sticks, etc., for spring.